Saint Dominic
AND THE ROSARY

Saints and Sacramentals Series

By Shaun McAfee
Illustrated by Jennifer Beam

TAN Books
Gastonia, North Carolina

Text used for reference: *The History of Saint Dominic*. Augusta Theodosa Drane, O.P. (1857).

Cover design and interior layout by Jordan Avery
Illustrations by Jennifer Beam

ISBN: 978-1-5051-3445-2
Kindle ISBN: 978-1-5051-3686-9
ePUB ISBN: 978-1-5051-3685-2

Published in the United States by
TAN Books
PO Box 269
Gastonia, NC 28053

www.TANBooks.com

Printed in the United States of America

"Arm yourself with prayer rather than a sword;
wear humility rather than fine clothes."

—St. Dominic

Author's Note

Have you ever dipped your fingers into holy water and made the Sign of the Cross? Or watched a priest bless a home with incense and prayers? These are called sacramentals—special signs and actions the Church gives us to help us grow closer to God.

A sacramental is something holy that reminds us of God's presence and prepares our hearts to receive His grace. Sacramentals are not the same as the seven Sacraments (like Baptism, the Eucharist, or Confession), but they help us to be ready for those big moments. You can think of sacramentals as little lights along the road that help guide us toward Jesus.

The Church has sacramentals because Jesus cares about our senses—what we see, hear, smell, and touch. He made us with a body and soul. That's why, during His life, He used things like water, mud, and even His own hands to heal and bless people. The Church follows His example by giving us holy things we can see and use to help us love God more.

Some sacramentals are objects—like holy water, crucifixes, blessed medals, rosaries, and scapulars. Others are actions—like blessings, prayers, or making the Sign of the Cross. When we use these things with faith, they help protect us from evil, remind us of heaven, and open our hearts to receive grace from God.

One of the most powerful sacramentals in the Church is the Rosary. It's more than just a string of beads—it's a prayer that helps us think about the life of Jesus through the eyes of His Mother, Mary. Many saints have loved the Rosary deeply and prayed it every day—but none so much as Saint Dominic, who you will meet in this book.

Sacramentals are beautiful gifts from the Church. They don't work like magic, but when we use them with love and trust in God, they help us grow in holiness and stay close to Jesus.

Around 800 years ago, a joyful woman named Joan walked almost every week to the mountainside near her home for prayer. She was from a small town in the countryside of Spain, called Caleruega. In this town, all the houses were made of stone from the nearby hills, which meant the people here were rugged and tough.

“Don’t you get tired from walking these hills every week?” a monk once asked Joan.

“It is a very long walk, but here at the monastery of Silos, I feel safe, warm, and confident in my prayers.”

“And what do you pray for?” asked the monk.

"I pray that my children, especially the one I am carrying, will be as gentle, as wise, and as holy as the patron of this great monastery, Saint Domingo of Silos. Indeed, I plan to name my child after our great patron saint."

Some weeks later, while she was visiting the monks again for prayer, she saw something truly glorious at the walls of the monastery.

A dog was there, and this dog held a torch in its mouth! It was running about, here and there, lighting all the fields, the hillsides, the cities—the whole world—on fire!

“What could this mean?” Joan thought, holding her pregnant belly.

At the baptism, his godmother, too, saw an awe-inspiring sign of the boy's great life to come.

"Look! A bright star has appeared on the child's head!" she exclaimed, just as the priest was pouring the holy water over the little baby.

Though Joan didn't understand the visions yet, she trusted God with her new child and chose to name the boy after Saint Domingo of Silos.

We know him as

Dominic

Dominic was born to a very loving home where Joan and her husband prayed daily and hoped for their children to remain lifelong Catholics.

Joan already had two boys who were preparing to become priests. Yet, Joan thought so well of this child that she wanted God to use him however He wished.

His parents would remind him often, “Remember the words of the gospel, that God loves you so much, and that He became man for the sole purpose of purchasing your soul with His suffering and death. He did this so that if you believe in Him, you will also rise on the last day and live with Jesus forever.”

As the years went on, Dominic attended schools and liked to ask questions about the Church. He made friends with nearly everyone he met, and no one ever left his company without having felt better for it.

Dominic decided to stay at the Benedictine monastery in Osma, where he could observe a religious way of life and continue his studies within the walls of the library. He was also able to journey to nearby towns for learning.

One day, the king asked the Bishop of Osma to take a trusted religious from within his community to a faraway land. The bishop chose his best canon, Dominic de Guzmán, and his mission was to bring back the hand of a princess for the king's son to marry.

But on their way, they stopped in a city in France named Toulouse, and Dominic met an innkeeper. This man worried Dominic because of his beliefs about God, the afterlife, and even the human body.

"I most certainly must help this man," said Dominic. Because the innkeeper had to spend all night watching over the inn, Dominic gave up his sleep to teach the man the Truths of God. By morning, the man was converted.

"Thank God you are here. But there are a great many others who believe these things, too," said the innkeeper. "You must return from your journey to preach here."

Before Dominic left to continue his journey the next day, he asked the innkeeper, "Where did you say the people who taught you these things were from?"

"From the city of Albi, just southwest of here."

Soon, Dominic and the bishop completed their mission, but what the innkeeper told him did not sit well in his heart. "If all those people are being taught incorrectly about Christ and even the earth we walk on, I must do something about it!"

So, Dominic set out to preach and became widely known for his charity and defense of the Catholic Faith against these false teachers from Albi—known as the Albigensians.

Although he preached well, Dominic still prayed constantly that God would help him preach with the right words and help him show these people a deep knowledge of God's love for them.

The Blessed Virgin Mary was a constant intercessor for Dominic. In his mind, God brought Jesus into the world through Mary—so why couldn't He bring Jesus to these people through Mary as well?

“Dearest Mother, please help these people,” he begged. “Please open their hearts to the Truth. Even though they are children of this false faith, I know that God loves them, and they are His children first.”

It was at this time, in the southern region of France, that the Blessed Virgin visited Dominic with a special message and devotion.

The Immaculate Mary, with three angels, appeared and asked St. Dominic, "Dear Dominic, do you know which weapon the Blessed Trinity wants to use to reform the world?"

Dominic replied that the Blessed Mary knew better than he, because she is a part of God's plan for our salvation.

Mary responded, "I want you to know that, in this kind of warfare, the battering ram has always been the Angelic Psalter which is the foundation stone of the New Testament. Therefore, if you want to reach these hardened souls and win them over to God, preach my Psalter."

"I will always preach the Psalter, my lady." And Dominic went about, widely preaching the composition of the Rosary and the mysteries revealed to him.

Word grew so much about his preaching that the local bishop invited him to instruct a group of women who were known to believe in the teachings from Albi. They lived in a little town called Prouille.

"Father Dominic, you cannot possibly teach us. We are already enlightened," one of the women said.

"Right! We already have teachers, and they provide for us!" another screamed at him.

Listening patiently, Dominic entered into a deep prayer which was disturbed by screaming.

“Father, look!” one of them shouted. A dark and hideous beast with eyes of flames walked right into their chapel. All of the women were stunned silent in fear.

But Dominic remained calm. “Get back, you Satan!”

For a moment, the women were still speechless, until they suddenly broke out in tears. “Oh Father Dominic! What was that?”

“This was a most vile form of the master you have served, seizing you with fear rather than the joy that comes from freedom in Christ.”

"Father," one of the quiet women began after they had all calmed down, "How should we begin to correct these false teachings?"

"Our Lady—" he started.

"You mean the Virgin Mary?"

"Yes. Our Lady has given me a wonderful inspiration. She was the first follower of Christ and did not leave His side in His moment of terrible suffering. And through her whole life she always points us to Christ who is the Truth."

The women leaned in to listen closely.

"Mary always points us to Christ. So, you must read the Scriptures and reflect on the life of Christ, and you must ask for Our Lady's intercession; focusing on these key moments in the life of Jesus will reveal the mysteries of the true Christian Faith."

"Pray the Rosary always."

From that day, the ten women committed themselves to a religious life under the care of their bishop and with the special devotion taught to them by Dominic, using a simple set of beads.

"A Hail Mary and the Our Father are so easy to say. Even saying five Our Fathers and fifty Hail Mary's only takes a short amount of time," said Sister Adelaide. And they all gladly agreed.

Sister Gentiana smiled while reciting the Joyful Mysteries. "Each of these helps me understand the Incarnation, that God really became man to save us and bring us to His heavenly kingdom."

She went on, "In **the Annunciation**, Mary is chosen to be the mother of Jesus. During **the Visitation of Mary to Elizabeth**, the mother of John the Baptist recognizes Mary as the mother of Our Lord, and even baby John the Baptist leaps for joy in Elizabeth's womb. For **the Nativity**, Jesus is born and laid in a poor manger and even the angels adore Him. In **the Presentation**, Joseph and Mary obey the Law of Moses, and Jesus is presented in the Temple at Jerusalem. **Finding Jesus in the Temple**, at his young age of twelve, must have required incredible trust in God, especially when they found Him answering questions there."

Knowing Our Lord chose to become man for the sake of dying for us is surely something to be joyful about!

"It is right to feel sorrow for His suffering, too" Sister Jordana said with a sad look on her face as she described the Sorrowful Mysteries.

"**The Agony of Jesus in the Garden** tells us about how Jesus prayed when confronted with the sins of the world—we must do the same. At **the Scourging at the Pillar**, Jesus is whipped almost to the point of death. After this, **Jesus is Crowned with Thorns**—although He is mocked, it portrays the beautiful humility of His work as Our Lord. **Jesus Carried the Cross** next, and this is a picture of Him carrying the weight of our sins. In the final mystery, **the Crucifixion of Our Lord**, Jesus Christ dies to save all mankind from sin."

The gift of salvation is the greatest gift we could ever receive. It is sad to think of how much Jesus suffered, but these sufferings make each of us sorrowful for our sins.

"I enjoy meditating on the Glorious Mysteries. These help me remember the amazing events that happened after His death and that the Resurrection is real," said Sister Adelaide.

"Jesus rises in victory over death in **The Resurrection**—a victory we share in Baptism and at the end of time. Just before Jesus's Ascension to Heaven, He trusts us with a special task to spread His love and message to the whole world. **The Descent of the Holy Ghost** at Pentecost means the Church is born.

The Assumption of Mary into Heaven marks the occasion when she was gloriously assumed into heaven as the first of the followers of Christ. Then, **Mary is Crowned as Queen of Heaven and Earth**, a true honor above all creatures!"

These mysteries tell us much about God's plan for mankind, that it is not just our spirit that matters, but that the body does, too.

This is why the Bible reminds us that the body is the Temple of the Holy Spirit. We do well when we take care of both!

Soon, the entire countryside was being taught how to pray with the string of beads, and the more the people from Albi considered the mysteries and the words of Scripture, the further their faith and love in Christ was deepened. Eventually, the errors of the people were corrected and Truth was restored.

Although it was officially known as Our Lady's Psalter, the faithful enjoyed creating more poetic names for various prayers. They saw this set of prayers as an arrangement of roses: fragrant, delicate, timeless, and beautiful. What they started to call the *rosarium* in Latin ("rose garden") became the Rosary today.

Word of Dominic's success with the Rosary quickly reached Rome, and sooner after, the pope approved of his mission to erase false Christian teaching through the prayerful meditations on the Mysteries of the Holy Rosary.

One day, the pope said, "You and your followers are not just named after you as the 'Dominicans'—they are the *Domini Cani*," the pope went on, "In Latin, this means 'Hounds of the Lord.'"

Hounds of the Lord

Popes through the centuries have continued to support the Rosary. Pope Saint John Paul II loved the Rosary so much that he said, “The Rosary is my favorite prayer. Marvelous in its simplicity and its depth.”

He also approved another set of mysteries known as the Luminous Mysteries or "The Mysteries of Light" which reveal to us the mission of Christ as "light of the world" (John 8:12).

The Baptism in the Jordan—God reveals that Jesus is His Son.

The Wedding at Cana—Jesus performs a surprising miracle at a wedding feast, at the prompting of His mother. This was his first public miracle.

The Proclamation of the Kingdom of God—Jesus teaches that the Kingdom of God will be brought to earth.

The Transfiguration— Jesus shows Peter, James, and John His divinity. He is gloriously transformed to a brilliant light, truly the light of the world for the three apostles to see.

The Institution of the Eucharist—Jesus shares His Body and Blood for our salvation and institutes the priesthood.

Dominic continued his work and attracted an enormous following. Within just fifty years, small groups of Dominican houses were seen all across the known world.

Truly, his mother Joan's vision had come true—the dog lighting the whole world on fire was her son, who had lit a flame in the hearts of men and women everywhere with love for the Lord and the Truth of Christianity.

The End

"You see the wonderful results I have had in preaching the Holy Rosary. You and those who love Our Lady **must do the same**."

—St. Dominic

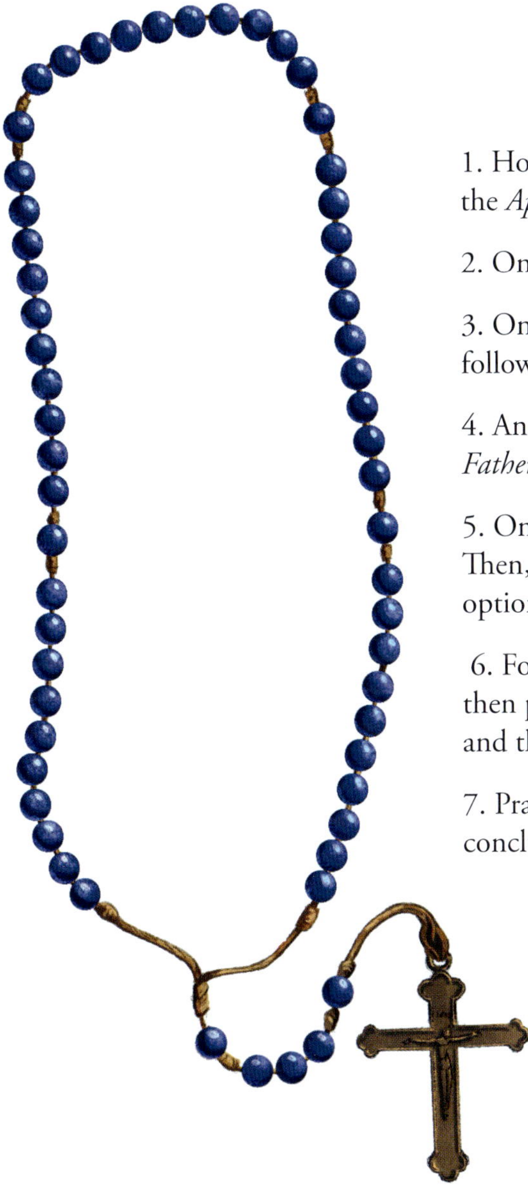

How to Pray the Holy Rosary

1. Holding the crucifix, make the *Sign of the Cross*. Pray the *Apostles' Creed*.

2. On the first bead, pray one *Our Father*.

3. On the set of three beads, pray three *Hail Mary's*, followed by a *Glory Be*.

4. Announce the first mystery, then pray one *Our Father*.

5. On each of the first ten beads, pray a *Hail Mary*. Then, on the bigger bead, pray a *Glory Be* and the optional *Fatima Prayer*

6. For each subsequent decade, announce the mystery, then pray one *Our Father*, ten *Hail Mary's*, a *Glory Be*, and the optional *Fatima Prayer*.

7. Pray *The Hail Holy Queen* and *The Rosary Prayer* to conclude the Rosary.

Prayers of the Rosary

The Apostles' Creed

I believe in God,

the Father almighty,

Creator of heaven and earth,

and in Jesus Christ, his only Son,
our Lord,

who was conceived by the Holy Spirit,

born of the Virgin Mary,

suffered under Pontius Pilate,

was crucified, died and was buried;

he descended into hell;

on the third day he rose again
from the dead;

he ascended into heaven,

and is seated at the right hand of
God the Father almighty;

from there he will come to judge

Credo

Credo in Deum,

Patrem omnipotentem,

creatorem caeli et terrae,

*et in Iesum Christum, Filium eius
unicum, Dominum nostrum,*

qui conceptus est de Spiritu Sancto,

natus ex Maria Virgine,

passus sub Pontio Pilato,

crucifixus, mortuus et sepultus;

Descendit ad inferos;

*tertia die resurrexit
a mortuis;*

ascendit ad caelos,

*sedet ad dextram Dei Patris
omnipotentis;*

inde venturus est iudicare

the living and the dead.

I believe in the Holy Spirit,

the holy catholic Church,

the communion of saints,

the forgiveness of sins,

the resurrection of the body,

and life everlasting.

Amen.

Our Father

Our Father, who art in heaven,

hallowed be thy name;

thy kingdom come;

thy will be done on earth
as it is in heaven.

Give us this day our
daily bread;

and forgive us our trespasses

as we forgive those who trespass
against us;

and lead us not into temptation,

but deliver us from evil.

Amen.

vivos et mortuos.

Credo in Spiritum Sanctum,

sanctam Ecclesiam catholicam,

sanctorum communionem,

remissionem peccatorum,

carnis resurrectionem,

vitam aeternam.

Amen.

Pater Noster

Pater noster, qui es in caelis,

sanctificetur nomen tuum;

adveniat regnum tuum;

*fiat voluntas tua sicut in caelo
et in terra.*

*Panem nostrum quotidianum
da nobis hodie;*

et dimitte nobis debita nostra

*sicut et nos dimittimus
debitoribus nostris;*

et ne nos inducas in tentationem,

sed libera nos a malo.

Amen.

Hail Mary

Hail Mary, full of grace,
the Lord is with thee;

blessed are thou among women,

and blessed is the fruit of thy womb,
Jesus.

Holy Mary, Mother of God,

pray for us sinners

now and at the hour of our death.

Amen.

The Glory Be

Glory be to the Father, the Son,
and the Holy Spirit;

as it was in the beginning,
is now, and ever shall be,

world without end.

Amen.

Fatima Prayer

O my Jesus, forgive us our sins,
save us from the fires of Hell, and lead
all souls into Heaven, especially those in
most need of Thy mercy.
Amen.

Ave Maria

Ave Maria, gratia plena,
Dominus tecum;

benedicta tu in mulieribus,

et benedictus fructus ventris tui,
Iesus.

Sancta Maria, Mater Dei,

ora pro nobis peccatoribus

nunc et in hora mortis nostrae.

Amen.

Gloria Patri

Gloria Patri, et Filio,
et Spiritui Sancto;

sicut erat in principio,
et nunc, et semper,

et in saecula saeculorum.

Amen.

Oratio Fatima

Domine Iesu, dimitte nobis debita nostra,
salva nos ab igne inferni, perduc in
caelum omnes animas, praesertim eas quae
misericordiae tuae maximae indigent.
Amen.

The Hail Holy Queen

Hail, Holy Queen, Mother of Mercy! Hail, our Life, our Sweetness and our Hope! To thee do we cry, poor banished children of Eve; to thee do we send up our sighs, mourning and weeping in this valley of tears. Turn, then, most gracious advocate, thine eyes of mercy toward us, and after this, our exile, show unto us the blessed fruit of thy womb, Jesus. O clement, O loving, O sweet Virgin Mary!

V: Pray for us, O Holy Mother of God

R: That we may be made worthy of the promises of Christ.

The Rosary Prayer

V: Let us pray

R: O God, whose only begotten Son, by His life, death and resurrection, has purchased for us the rewards of eternal life, grant we beseech Thee, that meditating on these mysteries of the most Holy Rosary of the Blessed Virgin Mary, we may imitate what they contain and obtain what they promise, through the same Christ, Our Lord.
Amen.

Salve Regina

Salve, Regina, mater misericordiae!
vita, dulcedo et spes nostra, salve!
Ad te clamamus exsules filii Hevae;
ad te suspiramus gementes et flentes in hac lacrimarum valle.
Eia ergo, advocata nostra, illos tuos misericordes oculos ad nos converte. Et Iesum, benedictum fructum ventris tui, nobis post hoc exsilium ostende.
O clemens, o pia, o dulcis Virgo Maria.

V. *Ora pro nobis, sancta Dei Genitrix.*

R. *Ut digni efficamur promissionibus Christi.*

Oratio Rosario

V: *Oremus*

R: *Deus, cuius Unigenitus per vitam, mortem et resurrectionem suam nobis salutis aeternae praemia comparavit: concede, quaesumus; ut, haec mysteria sacratissimo beatae Mariae Virginis Rosario recolentes. et imitemur quod continent, et quod promittunt, assequamur. Per eundem Christum Dominum nostrum.*
Amen.

The Joyful Mysteries

Pray on Mondays and Saturdays

The Annunciation

"And he came to her and said, 'Hail, full of grace, the Lord is with you!' And the angel said to her, 'Do not be afraid, Mary, for you have found favor with God. And behold, you will conceive in your womb and bear a son, and you shall call his name Jesus.'" (Luke 1:28, 30–31)

The Visitation

"And when Elizabeth heard the greeting of Mary, the babe leaped in her womb; and Elizabeth was filled with the Holy Spirit and she exclaimed with a loud cry, 'Blessed are you among women, and blessed is the fruit of your womb!'" (Luke 1:41–42)

The Nativity

"And she gave birth to her first-born son and wrapped him in swaddling cloths, and laid him in a manger, because there was no place for them in the inn." (Luke 2:7)

The Presentation

"And when the time came for their purification according to the law of Moses, they brought him up to Jerusalem to present him to the Lord (as it is written in the law of the Lord, 'Every male that opens the womb shall be called holy to the Lord')" (Luke 2:22–23)

The Finding in the Temple

"After three days they found him in the temple, sitting among the teachers, listening to them and asking them questions; and all who heard him were amazed at his understanding and his answers." (Luke 2:46–17)

The Sorrowful Mysteries

Pray on Tuesdays and Fridays

The Agony in the Garden

And he withdrew from them about a stone's throw, and knelt down and prayed, 'Father, if thou art willing, remove this cup from me; nevertheless not my will, but thine, be done.'" (Luke 22: 41–42)

The Scourging at the Pillar

"Then Pilate took Jesus and scourged him." (John 19:1)

The Crowing of Thorns

"And the soldiers plaited a crown of thorns, and put it on his head, and arrayed him in a purple robe; they came up to him, saying, 'Hail, King of the Jews!' and struck him with their hands." (John 19:2–3)

The Carrying of the Cross

"Then he handed him over to them to be crucified. So they took Jesus, and he went out, bearing his own cross, to the place called the place of a skull, which is called in Hebrew Gol'gotha." (John 19:16–17)

The Crucifixion

"After this Jesus, knowing that all was now finished, said (to fulfil the scripture), 'I thirst.' A bowl full of vinegar stood there; so they put a sponge full of the vinegar on hyssop and held it to his mouth. When Jesus had received the vinegar, he said, 'It is finished'; and he bowed his head and gave up his spirit." (John 19:28–30)

The Glorious Mysteries

Pray on Sundays and Wednesdays

The Resurrection

"And he said to them, 'Do not be amazed; you seek Jesus of Nazareth, who was crucified. He has risen, he is not here; see the place where they laid him.'" (Mark 16:6)

The Ascension

"So then the Lord Jesus, after he had spoken to them, was taken up into heaven, and sat down at the right hand of God." (Mark 16:19)

The Descent of the Holy Spirit

"And suddenly a sound came from heaven like the rush of a mighty wind, and it filled all the house where they were sitting. And there appeared to them tongues as of fire, distributed and resting on each one of them. And they were all filled with the Holy Spirit and began to speak in other tongues, as the Spirit gave them utterance." (Acts 2:2–4)

The Assumption

"For as by a man came death, by a man has come also the resurrection of the dead. For as in Adam all die, so also in Christ shall all be made alive." (1 Corinthians 15:21–22)

The Coronation

"And a great portent appeared in heaven, a woman clothed with the sun, with the moon under her feet, and on her head a crown of twelve stars." (Revelation 12:1)

The Luminous Mysteries

Pray on Thursdays

The Baptism of the Lord

"And when Jesus was baptized, he went up immediately from the water, and behold, the heavens were opened and he saw the Spirit of God descending like a dove, and alighting on him; and lo, a voice from heaven, saying, 'This is my beloved Son, with whom I am well pleased.'" (Matthew 3:16–17)

The Wedding at Cana

"His mother said to the servants, 'Do whatever he tells you.' Now six stone jars were standing there, for the Jewish rites of purification, each holding twenty or thirty gallons. Jesus said to them, 'Fill the jars with water.' And they filled them up to the brim." (John 2:5–7)

The Proclamation of the Kingdom

"Jesus came into Galilee, preaching the gospel of God, and saying, 'The time is fulfilled, and the kingdom of God is at hand; repent, and believe in the gospel.'" (Mark 1:14–15)

The Transfiguration

"And he was transfigured before them, and his face shone like the sun, and his garments became white as light." (Matthew 17:2)

The Institution of the Eucharist

"Now as they were eating, Jesus took bread, and blessed, and broke it, and gave it to the disciples and said, 'Take, eat; this is my body.' And he took a cup, and when he had given thanks he gave it to them, saying, 'Drink of it, all of you; for this is my blood of the covenant, which is poured out for many for the forgiveness of sins.'" (Matthew 26:26–28)

"We affirm that the custom of the family recitation of the Holy Rosary is a most efficacious means. What a sweet sight—most pleasing to God—when, at eventide, the Christian home resounds with the frequent repetition of praises in honor of the august Queen of Heaven! Then the Rosary, recited in common, assembles before the image of the Virgin, in an admirable union of hearts, the parents and their children, who come back from their daily work. It unites them piously with those absent and those dead. It links all more tightly in a sweet bond of love, with the most Holy Virgin, who, like a loving mother, in the circle of her children, will be there bestowing upon them an abundance of the gifts of concord and family peace."

—Pope Pius XII

"The Rosary is the most excellent form of prayer and the most efficacious means of attaining eternal life. It is the remedy for all our evils, the root of all our blessings. There is no more excellent way of praying."

—Pope Leo XIII

Further Reading

Dear parents, this *Saints and Sacramentals* book serves as an introduction both to St. Dominic and the beauty of the Rosary. It is our hope that this book will inspire you and your children to learn more about St. Dominic and about the gift of the Rosary. Further reading on these topics can be found on our website. Scan the QR code on the next page to get started.

The Life of Saint Dominic
Sr. Augusta Theodosia Drane

Dominican Saints
Dominican Novices, St. Catherine of Siena

Saint Dominic: Preacher of the Rosary and Founder of the Dominican Order
Mary Fabyan Windeatt

About the Author

Shaun McAfee usually enjoys reading and writing books for adults who venture to embrace the fullness of the Catholic Faith. But his six children and love for their budding faith has given him a passion for children's books, too. Shaun holds a Masters degree in Dogmatic Theology from Holy Apostles College and Seminary. He and his wife Jessica, and their beautiful kids currently live in the New Orleans area.

About the Illustrator

Jennifer Beam was born in Hershey, Pennsylvania and has coincidentally loved chocolate ever since. Jennifer has always enjoyed reading books. She has also learned a lot as an artist from working in animation, since she's worked on many short and feature films. She loves painting skies and clouds because her head seems to always be in them.

Other Books by Shaun McAfee

All Things Catholic: A Guide from A to Z

Compendium of Sacramentals: Encyclopedia of the Church's Blessings, Signs, and Devotions

20 Answers: Sacramentals and Relics

Epic Saints: Wild, Wonderful, and Weird Stories of God's Heroes

I'm Catholic. Now What?

20 Answers: Conversion

Inseparable: Five Perspectives on Sex, Life, and Love in Defense of Humanae Vitae

Social Media Magisterium

Reform Yourself!

St. Robert Bellarmine

Filling Our Father's House